The Ladybug
and Other Insects

Created by Gallimard Jeunesse
and Pascale de Bourgoing
Illustrated by Sylvie Perols

D0009005

A FIRST DISCOVERY BOOK

Cartwheel
·B·O·O·K·S· ™

SCHOLASTIC INC.

New York   Toronto   London   Auckland   Sydney

This is a ladybird beetle.
We usually call it a ladybug.
The ladybug is an insect.

Ladybugs are often
red with black spots.

Like all insects, the ladybug has six legs.

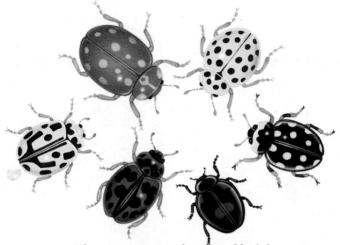

There are many kinds of ladybugs,
and they come in many
different colors.

This common ladybug has seven spots.

The
ladybug
has two
pairs of
wings.
Hard red
outer wings . . .

protect the
transparent
wings the
ladybug
flies with.

Like all
insects,
the ladybug
has three
body parts.

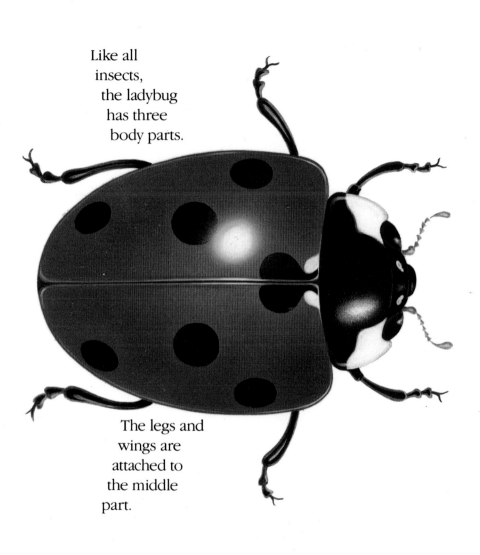

The legs and
wings are
attached to
the middle
part.

With its little claws and jaws, the ladybug
captures aphids — its favorite food.

One ladybug can eat as many
as fifty aphids in one day!

Near the ladybug's eyes are
two antennae, or "feelers."
The ladybug uses these to sniff out
the insects that it likes to eat.

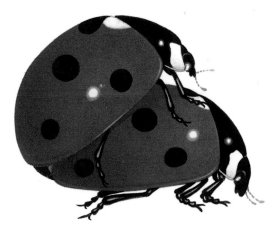

In the spring,
male and female
ladybugs mate
so the female
can lay eggs.

A week
later,
the female
finds a leaf
with many aphids
on which to lay
her sticky
yellow eggs.

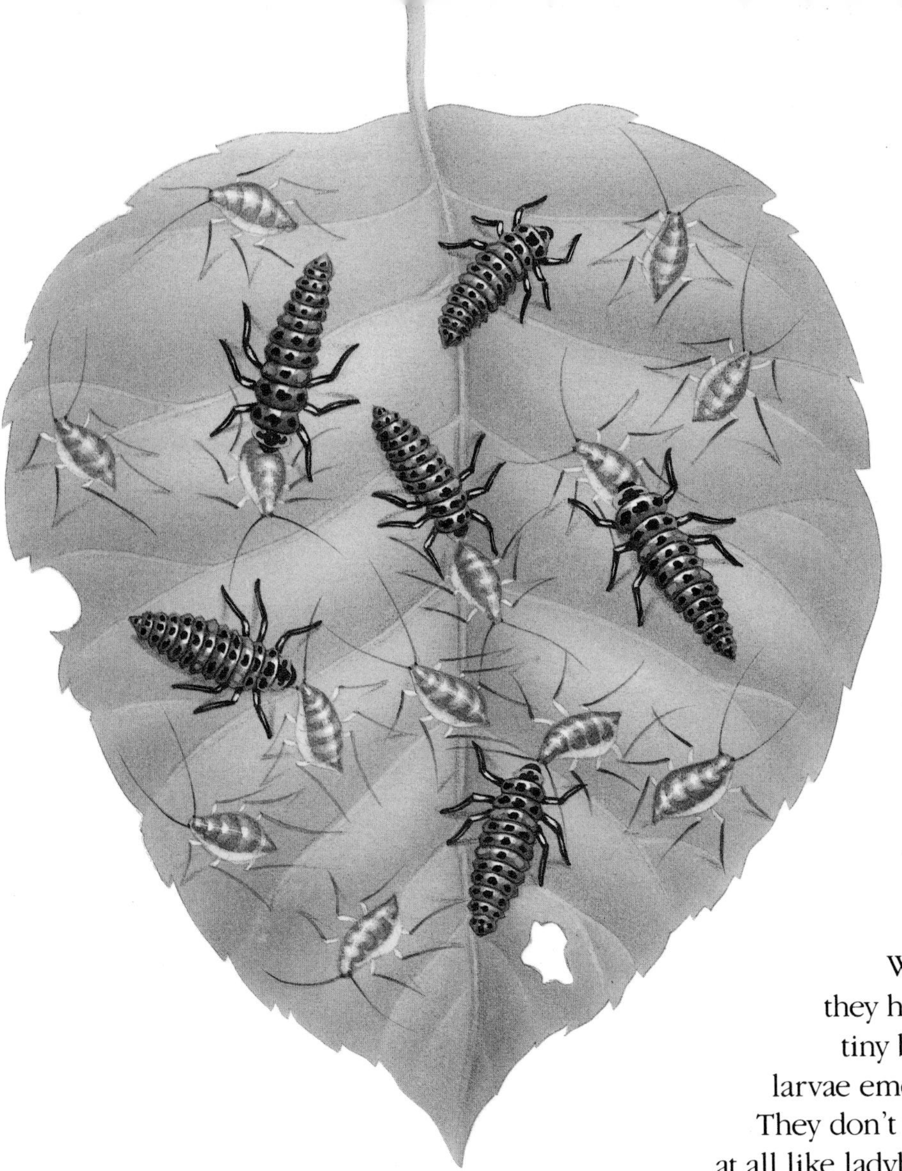

When
they hatch,
tiny black
larvae emerge.
They don't look
at all like ladybugs.
The larvae
feed on aphids.

A young larva eats and eats. As it grows,
it sheds its too-tight skin. When it is time
to change into a ladybug, the larva attaches
itself to a leaf. Its old skin splits off once more.
Now the larva is called a pupa. The skin
becomes a hard, dry shell. Inside this shell,
a ladybug is forming.

About a week
later, the ladybug
pushes out of the shell. Its
body is soft and yellow and
damp. Soon its outer wings
become dry and hard, and
turn red with black spots.

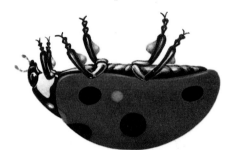

Some birds think
the brightly colored
ladybug looks
good to eat.
They soon find out
that they are wrong.
When a bird attacks,
some ladybugs
turn over,
become very still,
and excrete a
bad-smelling liquid
from their legs.

Many ladybugs
hibernate during
the cold winter months.

They find a warm, safe place
in the hollow of a tree
or under a pile of
leaves. They nestle
together and sleep
until the cold weather
is over.
Then when spring
arrives, they come
out to look for
a mate.

Let's look at some other kinds of insects.

This scarab beetle feeds
on cow dung. It rolls
balls of dung
between its strong legs.

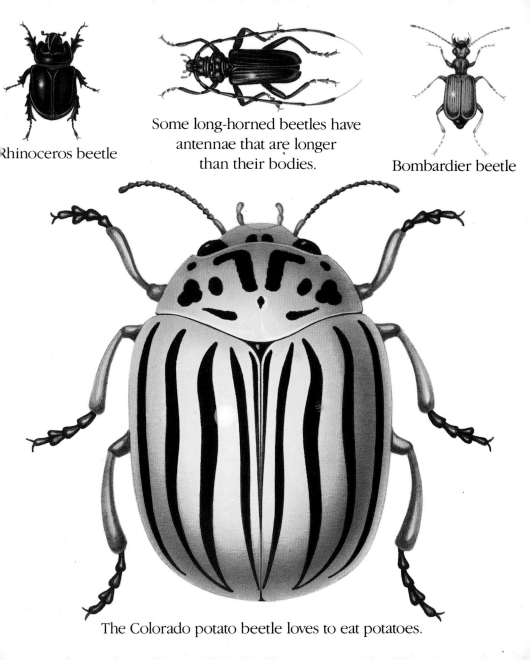

Rhinoceros beetle

Some long-horned beetles have antennae that are longer than their bodies.

Bombardier beetle

The Colorado potato beetle loves to eat potatoes.

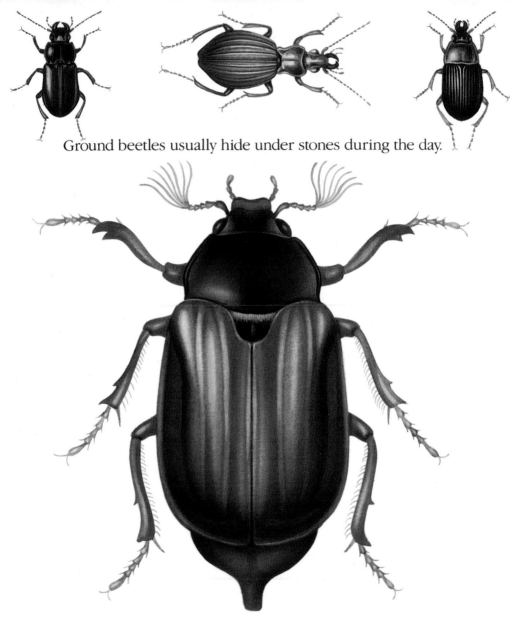

Ground beetles usually hide under stones during the day.

Most are brown, but some are brightly colored.

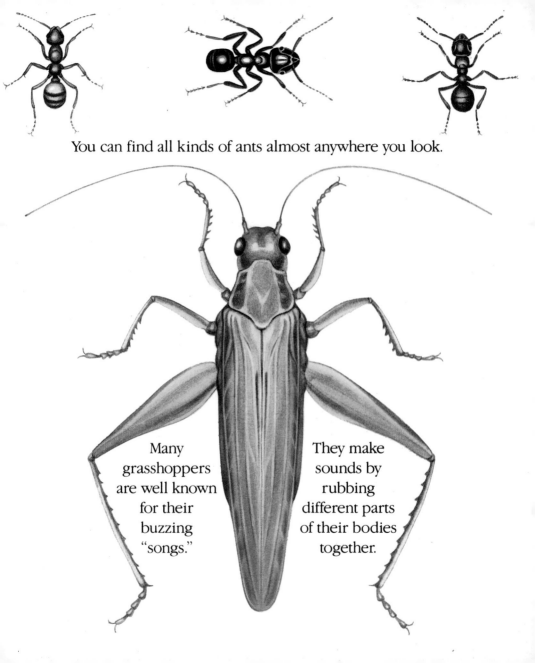

You can find all kinds of ants almost anywhere you look.

Many grasshoppers are well known for their buzzing "songs."

They make sounds by rubbing different parts of their bodies together.

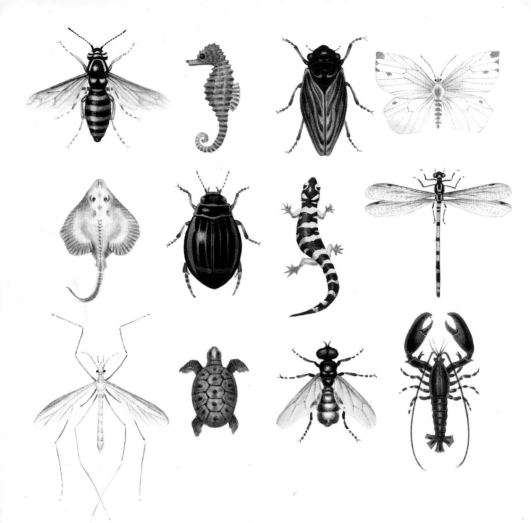

Remember that all insects have
six legs and three body parts.

Five of these animals are *not* insects.
Can you find them?

(Did you find a seahorse, a stingray, a salamander,
a turtle, and a lobster?)

What about these?
Are they insects?

(Snails don't have six legs
so they are not insects.)

Titles in the series of *First Discovery Books*:

Colors
Fruit
The Ladybug and Other Insects
Weather

Library of Congress Cataloging-in-Publication Data available.
Library of Congress number: 91-52891

Originally published in France under the title *La coccinelle* by Editions Gallimard.

ISBN 0-590-45235-5

12 11 10 9 8 7 6 5 4 3 2 1   1 2 3 4 5 6/9

Printed in Italy by Editoriale Libraria.

First Scholastic printing, October 1991